Words
To
Lift You

By

SUZETTE YATES-DAVIE

I would like to extend my sincere thanks to Mrs. Marsia Gray, and to my sister, Mrs. Maudie Yates-Khalifah, for proofreading the many materials I have written.

ISBN: 1-58597-217-7

Library of Congress Control Number: 2003114731

4500 College Blvd.
Overland Park, KS 66211
1/888/888-7696
www.leatherspublishing.com

Dedication

*First, to my Lord and Saviour, Jesus Christ —
You have inspired me to write each poem.*

*To my children, J'Ron and Sarronda, and to all
my brothers and sisters — these people have never
failed to believe in me.*

*Also, to Mrs. Margaret Cochran — who gave me
an opportunity to display my writing skills with
Christmas and Easter plays and poems for
church.*

Table of Contents

Words To Encourage Witnessing *(Continued)*

Words To Encourage a Mother 45

Words To Encourage a Father 57

Words To Encourage Personal Examination

This section of Words To Lift You will encourage you to examine your Christian life and to search the scriptures for eternal life.

Search the scriptures; for in them you think ye have eternal life: and they are they which testify of me.

— St. John 5:39

Sideline Christian

A sideline Christian is one who sits idly by,
watching precious and innocent souls die.

Never really getting in the Christian race;
moving at the same old selfish pace.

Pointing fingers at their fellow man;
not willing to lend a helping hand.

Calling plays from their comfort seat;
always ending up in self-defeat.

We cannot be sideline Christians in this race
if we plan to meet the Master one day face to face.

We must work and live according to the will of the
True Vine
and get off the defeated sidelines.

Prepare for That Day

We must prepare for that day;
Heaven is a place where only prepared people can go
and stay.

God prepared a ram in the bush for Abraham one day,
for Abraham's faith would not sway.

The Israelites prepared for their exit from Pharaoh's
harsh reign;
In the wilderness they lifted their voices to Him to sing.

John the Baptist prepared the way for Christ;
He pointed men and women to the "Light."

Jesus' body was prepared to suffer for us;
Through His suffering, dying and resurrection,
He made a way of escape for us.

We must be prepared for that day,
To hear the Master say:

"You have been faithful, my little one,
for the battles you have won.

"You have prepared yourself for this day,
Welcome, come in and stay!"

Our Christian Garment

We must wear our Christian garment each day,
no matter what situations come our way!

Avoiding sin which leaves the smallest dots,
keeping our Christian garment free from this world's
sinful spots.

Unforgiveness causes our Christian garment to
become old and to rot;
It causes our name from the Book of Life
to be blotted out.

Sin will stain us all;
It causes great men and women to fall.

The blood of Jesus washed our garments
white as snow;
If we humble ourselves to Him and pray,
Our Christian garment He will cleanse every day.

Daily Examination

We examine our physical appearance every day,
making sure we look a certain way.

Checking to see if everything is in place,
having the look of confidence on our face.

Appearing to be doing just fine;
Inside it is rainy, there is no sunshine.

We must examine ourselves daily from within,
making sure Christ lives therein.

We must examine our thoughts
And acknowledge our faults,
making sure they are right
in God's holy sight.

We must examine our conversations with every word
we utter,
showing true love to one another.

We must work with our hands,
doing God's master plan.

Our feet walking on the path of righteousness,
making our examination day victorious.

We must examine ourselves daily before Him,
so in our lives He can live therein.

God Will Change Our Name

When God comes into our heart,
sin and hatred will depart.

God will create in us a brand new change,
for our lives will no longer be the same.

God will bring forth a wonderful change,
if from sin we will refrain.

Our conversations and actions will not be the same,
for only Jesus' name we will proclaim.

God will give us a brand new life style,
if to Him we prayerfully bow.

God will take away all fear and shame,
for He will change our name!

In Search of a Gift

As I walked through the gift shop store,
all the precious gifts I did adore.

I searched high and I searched low.
Could I find the gift I was in search of on earth below?

A "What-Not" here,
A "What-Not" there,

Something was missing in that gift shop store.
I was searching for something much more.

The gift I was searching for would bring me
so much love, peace and joy,
a gift the whole world would come to adore.

When I opened the door of my heart,
sin and hatred, they did depart.

The Temple of God

God bought us with His special price,
so we can someday stand in His precious sight.

Our bodies were made for Him to live therein,
living righteous before Him until the very end.

When in our heart Christ lives inside,
sin and hatred cannot abide.

Our bodies are God's dwelling place;
In them sin should have no resting place.

We are the temple of the "True and Living God."
We must avoid things that displease Christ our Lord.

Reflections

When you look into the mirror, what do you see?
Is it a reflection of God or angry bees?

When you look into the mirror, do you see a frown?
Or is it a reflection of someone wearing
a heavenly crown?

The image that reflects back at you —
is it one that others would want, say or do?

Does it reflect love, joy and peace?
Or is it dirty, cloudy and smeared?

Your reflection goes wherever you go;
You must wear your Christian Reflection
so others may come to know.

Lifetime Commitment

We commit ourselves to our family and friends,
a commitment we say will never end.

We commit ourselves to our homes and careers,
to our loved ones both far and near.

God wants us to be totally committed to Him
in our daily service before women and men!

We must commit ourselves totally to the Lord,
in good times and when times
may seem to be a little hard.

From His love we should never stray,
nor depart from this Christian way.

God wants a lifetime commitment to Him,
even when life's pressures
seem to have no end.

Christian Luggage

Our Christian luggage should be packed
with love, joy and peace,
each compartment filled with prayers and praises
to God which shall never cease!

Our Christian luggage should remain packed
throughout each day,
as we travel along this narrow way.

Sin will weigh our Christian luggage down;
It will cause us to lose sight of our heavenly crown.

Inside our Christian luggage the fruit of God's spirit
should be packed,
not knowing when the enemy of God will try to attack.

Inside our Christian luggage God's fruit must abide;
His love will show forth on the outside
what's packed down on the inside!

We must pack our Christian luggage with God's love,
as we journey through this land
to our heavenly home above!

The Wages of Sin

Sin separates people from God's favor,
no matter what form of sinful flavor!

Sin separates love in families and friends;
Sin brings about a deadly end!

Sin will destroy the best of relationships;
It will bring about the lack of fellowship.

Sin should never be overlooked;
It causes the greatest men and women to become
bound and hooked!

Unforgiveness causes more sin to manifest;
It leads to destruction, death and lack of rest.

When we are forgiven of sin in our lives,
our hearts are open to God's love, joy and peace;
Our praises to Him shall never cease.

The wages of sin is death,
but the gift of God is eternal life.

We must choose life,
And put away all sin, hatred and strife.

Make Your Reservation

*We make reservations for many special events,
especially around the Day of Advent!*

*We seek places, which are comfortable
and prices that are affordable.*

*We make reservations days and years in advance,
not taking a last minute chance.*

*A confirmation number assures us of our space,
When we arrive at our destination place.*

*We must make our reservation now
for that Heavenly place,
so we can see the Master face to face.*

*Jesus Christ died to reserve a place for us,
if we accept Him as our Lord and Saviour
and refrain from the works of the flesh.*

Who Is Worthy?

Will you be worthy to stand before His throne?
On those streets will you roam?

Worthy to stand before His face,
to enter in that glorious place!

Do you long to see the Precious Lamb,
to bow before the Great I Am?

Make yourself ready for that day,
to hear the Master say:
"You have been faithful unto the end;
My child, thou art worthy to enter in!"

Words To Encourage During Hard Times

**This section of Words To Lift You
will encourage you to hold fast to your
Christian profession even when
the storms of life weigh heavy.**

*I can do all things through Christ,
which strengtheneth me.*
— Philippians 4:13

Don't Let Your Past Hold You Back

Our past lives may have had some days that were dark;
Sin may have left some stains and marks.

Satan tries to keep our past holding us back;
It is our future in God he wants to attack.

Our past will keep us feeling down;
It keeps us from aiming toward our heavenly crown.

We can no longer allow our past to hold us back.
God is directing and guiding our future;
In Him there is no lack.

The enemy wants to keep our past ever before us,
so we won't reach for the future God has planned for us.

When Satan, that old lying wonder,
comes to remind us of our past,
we must remind him of his future —
In the "Lake of Fire and Brimstone" will he be cast!

Don't let your past determine your future acts;
Don't let your past hold you back!

Road Blocks

Does it appear the road in which you are traveling
is blocked?
All exit ramps are shut down and traffic has stopped.

Satan will try to magnify those small rocks,
which lie in your pathway,
As large boulders and blockades on the roadway.

The children of Israel faced many roadblocks
along the way,
But God, "The Master Boulder and Blockade Remover,"
cleared their way.

No matter what roadblocks you might be facing today,
Remember God can remove all blockades away.

So as you travel on this Christian journey ahead,
Do not make any detours;
You have no roadblocks to dread.

For God is able to clear your road of all debris,
So you, His precious child, can clearly see.

The Break of Day

The break of day brings us light;
The sun shines so very bright.

The morning light calms our fears;
The melody of birds is music to our ears.

The light of day helps us see so much clear,
As we go throughout the days and years.

The light brightens up our path;
That's why God gave His Son on our behalf.

To bring the world His Guiding Light,
Which brought light to the dark of night.

So when His light shines our way,
Thank God for yet another day.

Be a beam of light in someone's sight,
And lead them to God's Guiding Light.

Special Delivery

God has special blessing stored up for us,
Blessings He longs to impart to us.

Special blessings all people can receive,
If in Christ Jesus we only believe.

A special delivery came into the world,
To every man, woman, boy and girl.

God gave us His very best;
Jesus is recommended above all the rest.

God pre-paid for our souls,
All nationalities, no matter how old.

His Son paid in full on the cross,
So no one would be lost.

God has a special delivery just for you,
In care of His faithful servant, YOU!

The Sunshine Will Come

Do problems and trials have you down?
Seems hope cannot be found?

Does it feel like everyone has turned their backs?
This is just the enemy's attack.

The storms of life only last for a little while,
Even though it seems as if they are mounting up in piles.

If you hold on through the night storm,
Fear not, nor be alarmed.

You must trust God and put the enemy to flight,
For theses storms only last throughout the night.

When the storm is over the sun will shine,
Because you kept the faith and hope in the True Vine.

Don't give up, the sunshine will come your way,
If you lean and depend on God each day.

There is sunshine on the other side of the storm,
When you take cover in God's protective arms.

Freed from Egypt

We all have Egypts that we go through;
There are some things in our lives
Which make us feel somewhat blue.

Things may cause our faces to frown,
Seems like hope is nowhere around.

God sent His Son to deliver
us from our Egypt conditions and state of mind,
So we can live free in His True Vine.

When God delivers our hearts and minds from our Egypts,
we should never look back and yearn,
For in our personal Egypts we should have surely learned.

Trust in God to bring you through your own Red Seas;
He'll bring you out victorious,
If with your life He is pleased.

Good News

Disturbing news headlines will bring sorrow
To small and large cities and towns.

Sorrow will bring the happiest person down,
When trouble is around.

Sorrow binds and bounds,
Seems as if there is no hope to be found.

God sent His Son to bring the world wonderful news,
News that would wipe away all sorrow and blues.

God's news lifts heavy and broken hearts;
It restores love and joy,
Which from His love we drifted apart.

God's news will lift up the sick;
It restores strength to the weak.

God gave His Son Jesus, as our good news,
News not only for a selective few.

But to all who accept His Son, Jesus Christ,
As Lord and Saviour for He is our Good News!

Words To Encourage Witnessing

**This section of Words To Lift You
will encourage you to witness to your family,
friends and people you meet on the street.**

*Go into all the world, and preach
the gospel to every creature.*
— *St. Mark 16:15*

The Word of God

The Word of God brings us life,
Not hatred, sin nor strife.

The Word of God heals the broken heart,
His Word of love to men we must impart!

The Word of God brings comfort to our souls;
It helps us speak of His Word standing bold.

The Word of God heals all hurt;
It delivers us from Satan's evil works.

The Word of God is comfort when we are feeling alone,
It ministers to us through the words of songs.

The Word of God gives us wisdom and knowledge,
If to His Son's love we acknowledge.

Led by God

We are led by God to share His message of love;
His love comes from heaven above.

Led to speak a gentle and kind word
To those who say they have never heard.

To bring a message of love to all we meet,
To all who are sick, weak and strangers in the street!

The things we do should glorify Him,
So others can learn to trust and live in Him.

God leads us to bring all people hope,
To those who seem they just can't cope.

To lead mankind to God's highway,
Where there is no hatred or sin on the pathway.

God leads us by our hand each day,
So we can please Him in every way.

Shout It Out

*Many unfortunate things are
happening in our world today,
But from His love we must not stray.*

*We must hold fast to our profession,
Living according to our Christian confession.*

*God is worthy to be praised;
Our voices to Him in song we are to raise!*

*Holy hands we must lift up before Him,
To praise Him with all that is within.*

*The earth is the Lord's and the fullness thereof,
Everything in it and all that dwells therein.*

*We must shout it out wherever we go,
So others may know,*

The day of the Lord is at hand!

The Antidote

Sin is like a plague which spreads
throughout every nation;
It flows from person to person.

The spread of sin is like a disease;
It's highly contagious and deadly
to those who don't believe.

Sin will destroy families and friends;
It brings forth a deadly end.

Without an antidote for the sins of this world,
Death would have come
to every man, woman, boy and girl.

There are many antidotes
to prevent communicable diseases today;
The only antidote for sin is Jesus, who paid the way.

Jesus is the antidote for sin's deadly pains;
Jesus is the antidote to cure sinful stains.

Appointed

God has appointed His children to teach and preach
To every lost soul we must try to reach.

He has appointed us to share His Word,
To those who say they have never heard.

To send forth a message of love to strangers,
To those who walk in the path of danger.

He has appointed us fishers of men,
To our family and friends.

We are appointed to do God's will,
To speak salvation, deliverance and praying for all
who need to be healed.

He has appointed us as laborers in the vineyard,
When we accept this appointment,
we will receive a heavenly reward.

An Open Door

Nighttime causes our cities to shut down,
When evil is lurking around.

Stores close in the early evening time,
Due to the increase in crime!

Doors may close in our faces,
When seeking resting places.

Jesus' door will never close;
That's why from the grave He arose.

He will enter into our hearts any time of day,
When we call Him to come our way.

God's door is always open
to children, women and men;
If we give God the key to our heart,
He will freely enter in.

God wants to abide in our hearts made of clay;
That's why He ascended on that day.

Jesus is an opened door — please let Him in!

Our Assignment

Our assignment is to encourage people
to come to Christ,
No matter what the earthly price.
Compel those who are lost,
to come for Jesus paid the ultimate cost.

Each day our assignment may get a little harder;
With Jesus as our "Instructor,"
We can go on a little farther.

Encourage those who are weak,
As you journey through the streets.

We must complete our daily assignment each day,
For tomorrow a new one will come our way.

Each of us has an assignment to do;
This is your assignment God has given you:
Compel men, women and children to come!

Spread the Word

Spread the Word by the things you do and say;
Spread the Word each and every day.

Spread the Word no matter
what men and women may say,
For Christ will return one day.

Spread the Word in your actions, words and deeds,
So mankind can hear and see.

Spread the Word through the streets near your home,
So others can come to belong!

Use your voice to spread God's Word,
So others can say they've heard!

Sound the Alarm!

Signs of Christ's return are near;
We must pray, be watchful
and listen with our spiritual ears.

Trouble and disaster seem to be everywhere;
We must trust in God for our sorrow He will bear.

God's Word tells us that destruction would come one
day;
We must not fear, but continue to pray.

Christ will return to take His people
to His heavenly home one day,
If from His love we will not stray.

We must sound the alarm — Christ is on His way!

Yield to the Call

Before the foundation of the earth,
Before the day our earthly birth.

God sanctified and ordained us for His call,
To teach and preach His Word of Salvation to all,

To denounce and root out sin,
For the souls of mankind He called us to win.

God has called us to plant His seed of love
in mankind's hearts;
To His instructions we must yield and never depart.

God will help us through testing times,
When Satan thinks he has us in a bind.

Gird up thyself for He has called;
Trust in Him and you won't fall.

God has made His people defense cities,
iron pillars and brazen walls,
If we would just yield to His call!

Publish His Word

There are great people in this world;
There are great men, women, boys and girls.

Great workers, preachers, doctors and leaders,
Singers, missionaries and teachers.

They are great for the things they do and say;
There are many great people in this world today.

God's Word says, "Those who publish His Word
are truly great;
We must publish His Word before it is too late.

Before Christ returns to earth on that unknown date,
To take us to His heavenly home,
So we can enter through the pearly gates.

We must publish His Word to everyone we meet,
Yes, even the stranger on the street.

God Is in His Watch-Tower

God sits high and looks low,
Beholding mankind on earth below.

He knows our every word,
Every kind and idle word has He heard.

He sees and hears all we do and say,
Throughout each day that comes our way.

Whether good or bad,
Spoken by a child, mom or dad.

Nothing can be hidden from God above;
He wants mankind to walk in His love.

Our lives are open books to Him;
He knows our beginning and end.

God watches us from His "Watch-Tower";
We must live by His saving power.

In love and peace with our fellow man,
That is what God commands!

America, Turn Back to God

America has moved so far from God,
Not recognizing Him as Lord and God above all.

Talk of Him in public places has been banned;
This is the enemy of God's plan.

Lord, you told us to tell your Word everywhere we go,
At home, school, work and play,
Throughout each blessed day.

America has turned to worship things that are odd,
Forsaking the True and Only Living God!

Nothing is hidden from God, who sits in heaven above,
Who is looking down on earth below!

God knows the secrets of our heart.
Has America's love for God's Word grown cold and
apart?

God wants America to turn back to Him,
To offer Him praises from all who lives therein.

The Message and the Messengers

God has called us to be His messengers,
To tell a dying world to
"Repent for the Kingdom of Heaven is at hand"
is our message.

As messengers we are to speak His Word in the ears of
women and men,
To people we come to befriend.

John the Baptist was a messenger
who came before Christ;
He told the people to
"Prepare themselves to meet the Christ,"
For the Kingdom of Heaven is at hand.

Jesus, the messenger of God,
Came saying,
"Repent for the Kingdom of Heaven is at hand,"
And do as my Father commands.

God's message to the world has remained the same,
Only the messengers have changed.

Our message is to compel those who are lost,
To come for Jesus paid the Ultimate cost.

His message is to be spoken to those who are heavy
laden and burdened down,
To come for Jesus can restore life to you again.

As messengers we are to share His Word
With those who are weary and restless,
To come to Jesus for He will give you rest.

The messengers of God are to speak His message
everywhere we go,
So others will come to know,
"Repent for the Kingdom of Heaven is at hand!"

Words To Encourage
a Mother

**This section of Words To Lift You
will encourage you to express your love to your
mother, grandmother, sister and aunt.**

*Blessed art thou among women,
and blessed is the fruit of thy womb.*
— St. Luke 1:42

A Mother's Recipe

1 cup of Fairness

1 cup of Patience

1 cup of Protection

1 cup of Kindness

1 cup of Gentleness

A pinch of Tender Kisses and Hugs,

Blended together makes a recipe of a Mother's Love!

A Mother's Hands

You cuddled me in your hands as a little tot;
Your hands washed my little socks.

You wiped the tears from my eyes;
You held my hand and walked by my side.

When I fell and scraped my knee,
Your healing hands were there for me.

Your hand brushed my hair;
Oh what, a delightful feeling was there!

As I grew and grew and grew,
Your hands were still there to see me through.

Mother, I will never forget your wonderful hands.

A Mother's Reflections

Mother, you are genuine;
Your love is so kind.

You are my friend;
You promised to go with me to the end.

You are my teacher;
God's Word you'll preach.

You are valuable as rubies, diamonds and gold;
Your words will never grow old.

When I look into the mirror, I see a reflection of
Your Beauty,
Your Thoughtfulness,
Your Faithfulness, too.
Oh, how I wish to be just like you!

A *Grandmother's Wisdom*

(Words to encourage Grandmothers)

Grandmother, you are so wise;
Thinking of you brings twinkles to my eyes.

Your understanding and knowledge
Can withstand any textbook in college.

Grandmothers are often right;
They are perfect in their grandchildren's sight.

Grandmothers teach their generations
how they are to look;
They teach their grandchildren
passages from the good book.

In time of trouble grandmothers are there
to see you through;
If only there were more grandmothers just like you!

Sister to Sister

(Words to encourage a sister)

As sisters we share a special bond;
The times we share are so much fun.

A sister's love is as pure as gold,
Far above rubies and riches untold.

We share not only childhood memories,
But the gift of motherhood with all its victories.

As mothers we face different challenges every day;
Oh, the things which come our way.

Some old things, some new,
Mothers can fix a problem with that special glue.

A sister's love, her children will embrace,
Her patience they will try to trace.
My dearest sister,
in my heart there you will always have a place.

A Mother's Dream

(Words to encourage a daughter)

A mother's dream will surely come true,
When she sees her daughter walking in a mother's shoe.

Yesterday it seems I cuddled you in my arms,
To protect you from all fear and harm.

You held my hand as we walked down the street;
I can still hear the pitter-patter of your little feet.

Now you are grown,
With a dear little family of your own.

You teach your children love,
Love that comes down from heaven above.

I see you as you guide your children
in the way they should go,
For all who behold and know.

My dream has come true;
My daughter, I see you walking in my shoes.

My Wife

(Words to encourage a wife)

You were sent from above,
To fill my life with abundant love.

Your love and patience you give so freely,
To our children and even me.

You fill our home with joy and peace;
This love you give will never cease.

You are gentle, kind and thoughtful, too;
I really do love you.

Your beauty exceeds diamonds, and gold,
Rubies and riches untold!

You are my queen;
To my eyes you bring a gleam!

My sweetheart, I really do love you!

A Single Mom

(Encouraging words for a single mother)

Some days you work until very late;
You have so much on your plate.

With the cares of family and career,
You still remain a dear.

Your family is at the top of your list;
Family time you dare not risk.

Your family you hold in high regards;
You do all you do with the help of the Lord.

All the things you do should bite into your time,
But you come out fighting at the front of the line.

I want you to know how much I admire
your strength and power;
You are your family's strong tower.

A Mother's Love

When life had me feeling down,
When problems seemed to be all around,
You were there!

When my eyes were filled with tears,
You were ready to lend a helping hand or an open ear;
You were there!

When things were not on my side,
You were standing there with your arms open wide;
You were there!

You remained faithful through the years;
You help calm all my doubts and fears.

You never fail to believe in me,
For there you would always be.

What you have was sent from above;
It's a true mother's love.

Words To Encourage a Father

**This section of Words to Lift You
will encourage you to express your love to your
father, grandfather, brother, uncle or pastor.**

Honor thy father.

— Luke 18:20

Our Family's Strong Tower

You rise early in the morning to go earn the bread;
You do this without heartache and dread.

Upon your face there is a smile,
Traveling down the road and over highways for miles.

We watch you as you journey into the distance;
In a blink of an eye you are home in an instance.

You are our family's strong tower;
You hold us together with your love and God's Power.

Your love is so true;
Each day you make us feel brand new.

A Grandfather's Smile

Grandfather, your smiles
Will stretches for miles.

For you see yourself in the way I talk
And the way I walk.

When you see me coming near,
I see your heart begin to race and cheer.

When I need you, you come in haste,
For you said, "There is no time to waste."

Grandfather, you are so dear;
Without you I would not be here.

Words To Encourage Your Pastor

You help the congregation grow;
This each member does know.

You teach us from God's guide;
You won't let anything slide.

Each member you handle with care;
With each one of us, God's love you share.

We are the sheep;
When you preach God's Word, you cause us to leap!

You are God's shepherd;
Teach us, lead us and guide us
through God's Holy Word.

Encourage My Uncle

Uncles are like dads,
They make you feel happy and glad.

They always remind you of your childhood memories;
They praise you for
your accomplishments and victories.

Uncle, you helped to discipline me;
You told me that I could be all I ever wanted to be.

To be around you is such a delight;
Uncle, you are awesome in my sight!

Remembering Dad

When I look back and think,
I realize you were our family link.

You provided us shelter, food and clothes;
You did it with just a short time to doze.

When I was younger, I thought this was your job,
But your children's love you dare not rob.

You stood strong and tall;
Your family you wouldn't let fall.

Dad, thank you for being there through the years;
Today, I honor you with this special cheer.

All Grown Up

(Words to encourage a brother)

When we were younger, you were so carefree;
When time for house work came, you would flee.

As I watched you grow over the years,
With many struggles, prayers and tears.

Not only have you matured,
But many problems you have come to endure.

You saturate your family with love;
This love is sent from above.

You care for your family and provide for them, too;
Brother, fatherhood looks good on you!

Brotherly Love

(Words to encourage your brother)

I am so fortunate to have a brother like you;
You are thoughtful, loving and caring, too.

One who lends an ear,
No matter what time or day of the year.

You are always ready to give brotherly advice,
Without a fee or costly price.

You know when I am sad,
You know what things make me glad.

There is no one on earth that compares;
Brother, I love this bond we share.

A Father's Arms

Father, your arms are so very strong;
They comfort me when I am feeling alone.

Your arms protect me when all hope seems to be gone;
They chastise me when my feet go to do wrong.

Father, from your arms I will not stray;
I promise to follow in your pathway.